The Women
Part One

A look at the lives of five women in Scripture

Linda Osborne

Unless otherwise noted, all Scripture quotations are from the NEW AMERICAN STANDARD BIBLE®, Copyright © 1960, 1962, 1963, 1968, 1971, 1972, 1973, 1975, 1977, 1995 by The Lockman Foundation. Used by permission.

Published by Catch the Vision! Press
909 E Palm Avenue, Redlands, CA 92374
ISBN-10: 0692695265
ISBN-13: 978-0692695265

CONTENTS

OTHER BOOKS/BIBLE STUDIES
BY THE AUTHOR

Called to Lead: Catch the Vision!
1 and 2 Timothy & Titus: The Final Letters
Acts: Church Alive!
Colossians: Christ Supreme
David: Shepherd of Israel
Ephesians: Blessed!
Exodus: Deliverance
Galatians: Born (again!) to Be Free
Genesis: Beginnings
James: Let's Grow Up!
John: The Gospel of the Beloved
Philippians: Unrestrained Joy!
Revelation: Seven Letters to Seven Churches
Romans: The Gospel According to Paul
Ruth: A Love Story
The Women: Part Two
The Women: Part Three
The Women: Part Four
and
Lunch-Hour Lessons: Revelation

PREFACE

We are beginning a journey through the pages of the Old and New Testaments where we will look into the lives of several of the women found there. In the process of your study, you will be personally challenged to look at each woman for yourself, considering her strengths and her weaknesses, her trials and her triumphs, and making personal applications along the way.

This will be a time of discovery! You will not only uncover new and interesting things about the characters you'll be studying, but you'll discover new things about yourself as well. Keep that word discovery in mind, because the lessons are written in such a way that the discovery process will be yours alone, as will the personal application in the end.

If you feel that this study becomes somewhat confrontational— that's okay! Isn't that what it's all about—our personal preparation by God to be and fulfill all that He has for us? As we move through these pages and these lives, we will find that this is His ultimate aim: you and me becoming more like Jesus!

CHAPTER 1
EVE

This week we will be looking at the life of Eve. Eve's story may be the most fascinating all! Follow the thread: In Eve we have the most breathtaking beginning—the first woman ever made, taken from the rib of man, fashioned by the very hand of God, and placed into Paradise where there was no sorrow, fear, doubt, shame, or pain. But the promise of the beginning fell short, lost in a moment, when the first woman became the first sinner, leading her husband to sin and bringing death and darkness to her once beautiful world. It seems as if the story would end there, *but God had a plan*. Eve's sin was covered, she was named mother of all the living, and the promise was given of One who would eventually redeem the world from the sin, death, and darkness Eve's sin had brought. We will begin today by looking at what Scripture tells us about Eve. *This is her story.*

Eve's story covers several chapters of Scripture. Read the following verses and summarize the events described there:

Genesis 1:26-28_____

_____

_____

_____

_____

_____

_____

_____

_____

_____

1

Genesis 2_____

_____
_____
_____
_____
_____
_____
_____
_____

Genesis 3_____

_____
_____
_____
_____
_____
_____
_____
_____

Genesis 4:1-2 and 25-26_____

_____
_____
_____
_____
_____
_____
_____

Her Manner

Who Is She?

" ... Giving all diligence, add to your faith virtue, to virtue knowledge, to knowledge self-control, to self-control perseverance, to perseverance godliness, to godliness brotherly kindness, and to brotherly kindness love." 2 Peter 1:5-7

Eve's name means "life-giving" or "mother of all who have life." Today we will be looking at the *character* of Eve. Consider the Scripture you have read on Eve's life (you may reread the portions that will help you today) and use the following words to describe her:

✣ *Her strength*

✣ *Her weakness*

✣ *Her influence*

✣ *Her perseverance*

Unfortunately, Eve's life is one that teaches us from a negative perspective. We learn from her mistake. Although we can imagine that Eve had many wonderful characteristics, being that she was made perfect and sinless in the beginning, the emphasis of her story will always be that she took of the fruit and ate, bringing misery and suffering not only to herself but to all mankind.

1. Look carefully at Genesis 3:1-7 and see if you can identify Eve's downward progression into sin:

✣ *First Eve …*

✣ *Next Eve …*

✣ *Then Eve …*

2. What did the words of the serpent do to Eve's concept of God?

3. Describe what you understand to be the *character* of God (give Scripture if you can).

4. Describe what you understand to be the *character* of Satan (give Scripture if you can).

Although we realize that Eve probably didn't recognize the devil in disguise, when the character of God came into question she should have immediately stopped listening, taken her eyes off the enemy and the forbidden fruit, and turned her eyes and her attention back onto what she knew about her good and loving God. That would have been her salvation—and that is ours. When the enemy begins to bring thoughts that make us doubt the goodness of God, the minute we recognize what is happening we must stop listening to him and turn our thoughts and attention to God, remembering what we know to be true of Him.

5. How would the instruction found in James 4:7 have helped Eve in her day of temptation?

6. Does this verse bring you encouragement today?

Her Hope

"And blessed is she who believed that there would be a fulfillment of what had been spoken to her by the Lord." Luke 1:45

Today we will focus in on Eve's *hope*. From what you have studied about her this week:

✤ What was her *need*?

✤ What was her *hope*?

✤ What was God's *promise*?

Two of the most amazing and promising words throughout Scripture are the words, *"But God."* And, although we don't read those exact words in our story this week, they are certainly implied. Eve's sin brought darkness, sin, and death into a world where there had been only beauty, life, and light. Was all lost? It would have been, *but God* had a plan. The first words of His plan were spoken even as the judgment was handed out. To the serpent, who was Satan, God said, *"And I will put enmity between you and the woman, and between your seed and her Seed; He shall bruise your head, and you shall bruise His heel"* (Genesis 3:15). And thus we have the first promise of a Savior.

5

Two more promises of hope came for Eve. Share what you see as her hope from these verses in Genesis 3:

verse 20

verse 21

When Eve sinned, it must have seemed as if all hope was gone. But God judged her sin and then covered it, and pointed her to the future. The same will always be true for us.

1. Did Eve just fade away after she had sinned? See if you can recognize the difference it made for us that she continued on.

2. When you realize you have sinned, repented, and been forgiven by God, what do you need to do and why? Consider Jeremiah 29:11

Your Discovery

"Call to Me, and I will answer you, and I will tell you great and mighty things, which you do not know." Jeremiah 33:3

Sometimes when we do a study considering a character of the Bible, we start with a pre-conceived notion of who we think that person is. We have heard messages or read books about them. We already think we know them! We may have pre-set ideas based on the way they have been portrayed to us through the eyes of others.

Hopefully this week some of your pre-conceived notions have been changed, as you have looked at our subject with fresh eyes, seeking the Lord for a fresh glimpse of truth. Today we will look at what *you* have discovered or rediscovered about our woman of the week.

1. Did you have any pre-conceived notions about Eve? What were they?

2. Share at least one discovery or rediscovery you made about Eve in your study this week.

3. How did this change your thoughts about her or her circumstances?

4. Is there anything that you will think or do differently as a result of what you have learned from Eve?

5. Did you discover anything new about *yourself* this week? If so, what was it?

Your Prayer

"Search me, O God, and know my heart ..." Psalm 139:23

Compose a prayer to the Lord based on what you have gleaned from your study this week. Consider this: Is there anything you want to change in your life? Is there an attitude you realize needs adjusting? Is there a perspective that needs to be changed? Do you need to die to yourself? Do you need God's love poured into your heart for someone? Share whatever your heart is sensing with your Father in heaven who loves you and desires nothing more than to help you in your endeavor to be a godly woman.

_____

_____

_____

_____

_____

_____

_____

_____

_____

_____

_____

_____

_____

_____

_____

_____

_____

_____

_____

_____

_____

_____

NOTES

CHAPTER 2
MARY

✠

"Now the birth of Jesus Christ was as follows: After His mother Mary was betrothed to Joseph, before they came together, she was found with child of the Holy Spirit" (Matthew 1:18). What could be more incredible than the verse we have just read? It is a statement written in such simplicity, and yet relaying the most amazing message ever told. Jesus Christ, the promised Savior, born of a virgin by the power of the Holy Spirit. And that young virgin is Mary, the subject of our lesson this week. We will begin by looking at what Scripture tells us about Mary. *This is her story.*

Read the verses listed below and summarize the events described there:

Luke 1:26-56_____

_____

_____

_____

_____

_____

_____

_____

_____

_____

_____

_____

_____

_____

Matthew 1:18-25 _____

_____

_____

_____

_____

_____

_____

_____

_____

_____

_____

_____

_____

_____

Luke 2:1-19 _____

_____

_____

_____

_____

_____

_____

_____

_____

_____

_____

_____

_____

_____

_____

_____

_____

Matthew 2:1-23_____

_____

_____

_____

_____

_____

_____

_____

_____

_____

_____

_____

_____

_____

_____

_____

_____

_____

_____

Her Manner

Who Is She?

"... Giving all diligence, add to your faith virtue, to virtue knowledge, to knowledge self-control, to self-control perseverance, to perseverance godliness, to godliness brotherly kindness, and to brotherly kindness love." 2 Peter 1:5-7

Mary's name means "bitterness."

It doesn't seem right that this sweet young maiden's name would mean bitterness ... or does it? Although we see that Mary is the favored one of God and that she is the most blessed of women, we also see her as the one whose soul would be pierced with a sword (Luke 2:35), not once but many times.

Today we will be looking at the *character* of Mary. Considering the Luke 1 account of Mary's story, use the following words to describe her:

- *Her strength*

- *Her weakness*

- *Her humility/yieldedness*

1. From Luke 1:26-27, share what you know about Mary.

2. Is there anything in this list of facts that indicates why she was the one chosen to bear the Son of God?

3. What truth are we given in I Samuel 16:7?

4. What kind of a person might *we* have chosen to bring the most holy Son of God into this world?

5. What kind of person did God choose?

6. How did Mary's *character* make a difference in the way she handled her difficult situation?

7. What do you learn from Mary?

Her Hope

"And blessed is she who believed that there would be a fulfillment of what had been spoken to her by the Lord." Luke 1:45

Considering the incredible announcement made to Mary by the angel Gabriel:

✤ What was her *need*?

✤ What was her *hope*?

✤ What was God's *promise*?

As previously stated, Elizabeth's pregnancy was a sort of forerunner to the miraculous pregnancy of Mary. Elizabeth's pregnancy was actually a sign to Mary. Mary's question in Luke 1 was, *"How can this be, since I do not know a man?"*

Gabriel not only gave her an explanation, *"The Holy Spirit will come upon you, and the power of the Highest will overshadow you ..."* but a sign, *"Now indeed, Elizabeth your relative has also conceived a son in her old age; and this is now the sixth month for her who was called barren,"* and then the promise: *"For with God nothing will be impossible."* Luke 1:34-37 NKJV

1. What is the impossible thing in your life today? (If it is too personal to record here, make a mental note or note and date it elsewhere for future reference.)

2. Would it take a miracle for this thing to be done?

Oswald Chambers has said, *"The thing that taxes almightiness is the very thing which we as disciples of Jesus ought to believe He will do."*

3. Do you believe that our God is Almighty? What do Jeremiah 32:17 and 27 say about the power of God?

4. Mary's response to Gabriel was, "... may it be done to me according to your word" (Luke 1:38). Can you say this to God in regard to the impossible thing in your life?

5. How did Mary's surrender prove that her faith was in God alone?

Your Discovery

"Call to Me, and I will answer you, and I will tell you great and mighty things, which you do not know." Jeremiah 33:3

Today we will look at what *you* have discovered or rediscovered about our woman of the week.

1. Did you have any pre-conceived notions about Mary? What were they?

2. Share at least one discovery or rediscovery you made about Mary in your study this week.

3. How did this change your thoughts about her or her circumstances?

4. Is there anything that you will think or do differently as a result of what you have learned from Mary?

5. Did you discover anything new about *yourself* this week? If so, what was it?

Your Prayer

"Search me, O God, and know my heart ..." Psalm 139:23

Compose a prayer to the Lord based on what you have gleaned from your study this week. Consider this: Is there anything you want to change in your life? Is there an attitude you realize needs adjusting? Is there a perspective that needs to be changed? Do you need to die to yourself? Do you need God's love poured into your heart for someone? Share whatever your heart is sensing with your Father in heaven who loves you and desires nothing more than to help you in your endeavor to be a godly woman.

_____

_____

_____

_____

_____

_____

_____

_____

_____

_____

_____

_____

_____

_____

_____

_____

_____

_____

NOTES

CHAPTER THREE
RAHAB

❧

The story of Rahab gives us one of our greatest clues to the fact that God honors faith and that He is a God of grace. Rahab was a prostitute! But, when she put her faith in God and acted on that faith by helping His people, God saved not only Rahab but also her entire family. There are two highly notable things about Rahab: 1) She is included in the lineage of Jesus Christ; and 2) She is one of only two women mentioned in the Hebrews Hall of Faith. We will begin by looking at what Scripture tells us about Rahab. *This is her story.*

This week's study will require a lot of reading! We will be looking at Joshua 2 & 6. Read the following verses and summarize the events described there:

Joshua 2
verses 1-6_____

_____

_____

_____

_____

_____

_____

_____

_____

_____

_____

_____

_____

verses 7-14_____

_____

_____

_____

_____

_____

_____

_____

_____

_____

verses 15-21_____

_____

_____

_____

_____

_____

_____

_____

verses 22-24_____

_____

_____

_____

_____

_____

_____

_____

_____

Joshua 6

verses 1-5 _____

_____

_____

_____

_____

_____

_____

_____

_____

verses 15-17 _____

_____

_____

_____

_____

_____

_____

_____

verses 21-25 _____

_____

_____

_____

_____

_____

_____

_____

_____

_____

Her Manner

Who Is She?

"... Giving all diligence, add to your faith virtue, to virtue knowledge, to knowledge self-control, to self-control perseverance, to perseverance godliness, to godliness brotherly kindness, and to brotherly kindness love." 2 Peter 1:5-7

Rahab's name means "storm," "arrogance," "broad," or "spacious."

Today we will be looking at the *character* of Rahab. We know that she was a Gentile, and we know that she was a prostitute. From the Joshua 2 account, use the following words to describe her:

✤ *Her strength*

✤ *Her weakness*

✤ *Her courage*

✤ *Her influence*

1. Rahab was a prostitute who came to believe in the God of Israel and who acted on that belief by aiding Israel in taking the sinful Jericho. She could never go back and change the fact that she had been a prostitute, and Scripture never tries to cover up that fact. Although she couldn't change her past, considering 2 Peter 1:5-7, what *could* Rahab do?

2. In practical terms, what does this mean?

3. 2 Peter 1:8 says, *"For if these things are yours and abound, you will be neither barren nor unfruitful in the knowledge of our Lord Jesus Christ."* Consider Matthew 1:1-6a, and share the fulfillment of this promise in Rahab's life.

4. What does Rahab's salvation and her part in God's plan of redemption teach us? 1 Corinthians 1:26-29

5. What does Rahab teach *you*?

Her Hope

"And blessed is she who believed that there would be a fulfillment of what had been spoken to her by the Lord." Luke 1:45

From what you have studied about Rahab this week:

✤ What was her *need*?

✤ What was her *hope*?

✤ What was God's *promise*?

Rahab's testimony is not unlike most of ours. Look at Joshua 2:9-11 and share her testimony using her own words:

✤ What did she *know*? v. 9

✤ What did she *hear*? v. 10

✤ What did she *believe*? v. 11

1. Romans 10:9-10 and 17 give a sort of formula for salvation. See if you can connect these verses to Rahab's testimony.

2. When Rahab sent the spies off, she immediately put the scarlet cord in her window and began gathering her family together so that none would be lost. How does Hebrews 7:25 (speaking of our Savior) add depth and width, breadth and height to the promise of salvation offered to Rahab, her family—and to us?

One of the lessons that comes through Rahab's story perhaps like no other is that salvation is not dependent on human goodness— but rather on God's abundant and abounding grace!

✣ One commentator put it this way: "The deeper the need, the greater the grace."

✣ God's Word puts it this way: "But where sin abounded, grace abounded much more ..." (Romans 5:20b).

✣ A 19th century hymn writer put it this way: "His love has no limit; His grace has no measure; His pow'r has no boundary known unto men. For out of His infinite riches in Jesus, He giveth and giveth and giveth again!" --Annie Johnson Flint

3. What was your need when you first *heard* of Jesus?

4. Are you in need of grace today? Share with God your need and ask Him for His grace.

Your Discovery

"Call to Me, and I will answer you, and I will tell you great and mighty things, which you do not know." Jeremiah 33:3

Sometimes when we do a study considering a character of the Bible, we start with a pre-conceived notion of who we think that person is. We have heard messages or read books about them. We already think we know them!

We may have pre-set ideas based on the way they have been portrayed to us through the eyes of others. Hopefully this week some of your pre-conceived notions have been changed, as you have looked at our subject with fresh eyes, seeking the Lord for a fresh glimpse of truth. Today we will look at what *you* have discovered or rediscovered about our woman of the week.

1. Did you have any pre-conceived notions about Rahab? What were they?

2. Share at least one discovery or rediscovery you made about Rahab in your study this week.

3. How did this change your thoughts about her or her circumstances?

4. Is there anything that you will think or do differently as a result of what you have learned from Rahab?

5. Did you discover anything new about *yourself* this week? If so, what was it?

Your Prayer

"Search me, O God, and know my heart ..." Psalm 139:23

Compose a prayer to the Lord based on what you have gleaned from your study this week. Consider this: Is there anything you want to change in your life? Is there an attitude you realize needs adjusting? Is there a perspective that needs to be changed? Do you need to die to yourself? Do you need God's love poured into your heart for someone?

Share whatever your heart is sensing with your Father in heaven who loves you and desires nothing more than to help you in your endeavor to be a godly woman.

_____

_____

_____

_____

_____

_____

_____

_____

_____

_____

_____

_____

_____

_____

_____

_____

_____

_____

_____

_____

_____

_____

_____

_____

_____

_____

_____

_____

NOTES

CHAPTER FOUR
WOMEN WHO SERVED

❖

This week we will be looking at the stories of six women whose lives were unique, yet who had one thing in common—they loved and served their Savior. Service is the heart's response of gratitude and love. As we look at these women, we will see that service is not one-dimensional nor is it necessarily easily defined. It comes in many shapes and sizes—just like we do! We will begin today by looking at what Scripture tells us about these women. *This is their story.*

Following the name of each woman listed, read the verses given and summarize the events described there:

Anna
Luke 2:21-22 with 36-38 _____

_____

_____

_____

_____

_____

_____

Dorcas
Acts 9:36-42 _____

_____

_____

_____

_____

_____

_____

Lois and Eunice
Acts 16:1-2; 2 Timothy 1:5; 3:14-15_____

_____

_____

_____

_____

_____

_____

_____

_____

_____

Lydia
Acts 16:9-15, 40_____

_____

_____

_____

_____

_____

_____

_____

_____

Priscilla
Acts 18:1-3, 18-19, 24-28_____

_____

_____

_____

_____

_____

_____

_____

_____

Romans 16:3-5_____

_____

_____

_____

_____

_____

_____

_____

Her Manner

Who Is She?

"… Giving all diligence, add to your faith virtue, to virtue knowledge, to knowledge self-control, to self-control perseverance, to perseverance godliness, to godliness brotherly kindness, and to brotherly kindness love." 2 Peter 1:5-7

Today we will be looking at the *character* of each of the women we are studying this week. Reread each woman's Scripture passage and use the following words to describe her:

Anna's name means "favor" or "grace."

✤ *Her strength*

✤ *Her weakness*

Dorcas' name means "gazelle."

✤ *Her strength*

✤ *Her weakness*

Lois' name means "agreeable" or "desirable;" Eunice's name means "conquering well."

✤ *Their strengths*

✤ *Their weaknesses*

Lydia's name means "bending."

✤ *Her strength*

✤ *Her weakness*

Priscilla's name means "worthy" or "venerable."

✤ *Her strength*

✤ *Her weakness*

1. Which of today's characters do you most admire and why?

2. Do you have any similarities to this woman?

3. What might you need to do to be more like her?

Her Hope

"And blessed is she who believed that there would be a fulfillment of what had been spoken to her by the Lord." Luke 1:45

Today we're going to consider just one of our godly women in regard to her *hope*. We will be looking at *Anna*. Anna's story comes to us in the midst of the story of Mary, Joseph, and the baby Jesus.

When the time came for Jesus to be presented to the Lord in Jerusalem, there were two significant people present in the temple that day: The first was Simeon, a just and devout man who was waiting for the consolation of Israel or, in other words, the Messiah. On that very day he was led by the Spirit to the temple and saw with his own eyes the answer to his longing heart, the baby Jesus, the Messiah of God.

The second significant person was Anna the prophetess, the widow who never left the temple but served God night and day with fastings and prayers.

The Bible tells us that Anna came in that instant--in the same instant that Mary and Joseph were presenting Jesus to God, and in that same instant that Simeon held Him in his arms and prophesied over Him.

1. What two things are we told Anna did when she saw the baby Jesus? Luke 2:38

In light of the darkness of that time and Anna's hope for her people, we look at Anna the individual: (You'll need to put your thinking caps on!)

✤ What was her *need*?

✢ What was her *hope*?

✢ What was God's *promise*?

2. Why do you think Anna and Simeon were included in the privileged few that saw the baby Jesus and recognize Him as Messiah?

In the midst of the darkness of *his* day and his own personal suffering, the righteous Job expressed his hope with these words in Job 19:25 NKJV: *"For I know that my Redeemer lives."* And he went on to say in verse 27: *"Whom I shall see for myself and my eyes shall behold and not another. How my heart yearns within me!"*

Are you looking for Jesus? Do you expect to see Him—if not in this world, in the future resurrection? Job believed he would see his Savior. Anna and Simeon were present for His advent. We look toward His second coming. The point is we should be waiting, hoping, looking, and believing ...*"For the Scripture says, 'Whoever believes in Him will not be disappointed.'"* Romans 10:11

Your Discovery
"Call to Me, and I will answer you, and I will tell you great and mighty things, which you do not know." Jeremiah 33:3

Sometimes when we do a study considering a character of the Bible, we start with a pre-conceived notion of who we think that person is. We have heard messages or read books about them. We already think we know them!

We may have pre-set ideas based on the way they have been portrayed to us through the eyes of others. Hopefully this week some of your pre-conceived notions have been changed, as you have looked at our subject with fresh eyes, seeking the Lord for a fresh glimpse of truth. Today we will look at what *you* have discovered or rediscovered about our woman of the week.

1. Did you have any pre-conceived notions about any of the women we studied this week? What were they?

2. Share at least one discovery or rediscovery you made about a woman who served.

3. How did this change your thoughts about her or her circumstances?

4. Is there anything that you will think or do differently as a result of what you have learned from the women who served?

5. Did you discover anything new about *yourself* this week? If so, what was it?

Your Prayer

"Search me, O God, and know my heart ..." Psalm 139:23

Compose a prayer to the Lord based on what you have gleaned from your study this week. Consider this: Is there anything you want to change in your life? Is there an attitude you realize needs adjusting? Is there a perspective that needs to be changed? Do you need to die to yourself? Do you need God's love poured into your heart for someone? Share whatever your heart is sensing with your Father in heaven who loves you and desires nothing more than to help you in your endeavor to be a godly woman.

_____

_____

_____

_____

_____

_____

_____

_____

_____

_____

_____

_____

_____

_____

_____

_____

_____

_____

_____

_____

NOTES

CHAPTER FIVE
MIRIAM

❧

Miriam was born into the priestly tribe of Levi, the eldest child of godly parents. As sister of Aaron, the first high priest of Israel, and Moses, Israel's most famous leader, Miriam was a woman of prominence and leadership. We see her first as a helpful and very clever child, next as a commanding and influential leader, and finally as a discontented older woman. Miriam is another example of the heroes and heroines of the Bible failing as they enter into middle and old age. We should see this as a warning in our own walk with God to be ever on the alert and keep short accounts with Him always. Remember the word: An unguarded strength is a double weakness. We will begin today by looking at what Scripture tells us about Miriam. *This is her story.*

Read the following verses and summarize the events described there:

Exodus 2:1-10_____

_____

_____

_____

_____

_____

_____

_____

_____

_____

Exodus 15:20-21_____

_____
_____
_____
_____
_____
_____
_____
_____
_____

Numbers 12:1-15_____

_____
_____
_____
_____
_____
_____
_____
_____
_____
_____

Her Manner

Who Is She?

"… Giving all diligence, add to your faith virtue, to virtue knowledge, to knowledge self-control, to self-control perseverance, to perseverance godliness, to godliness brotherly kindness, and to brotherly kindness love." 2 Peter 1:5-7

Miriam's name means "bitterness."

Today we will be looking at the *character* of Miriam. Consider the Scripture you have read on Miriam's life and use the following words to describe her:

✤ *Her strength*

✤ *Her weakness*

✤ *Her influence*

✤ *Her ambition*

1. What do you learn from Miriam's *character* in her younger days, as a child?

2. What do you learn from Miriam's *character* as a leader of women?

Miriam's life began so well, only to end so sadly. The spirit of discontentment crept in and put an end to her ability to lead and influence others in a godly manner. In fact, Miriam became one who sowed discord.

3. In what way does Miriam's fall from grace warn you in your own walk with the Lord?

4. What kinds of *character* decisions might you make today to be sure *not* to follow in her steps?

Her Hope

"And blessed is she who believed that there would be a fulfillment of what had been spoken to her by the Lord." Luke 1:45

Today we will focus in on Miriam's *hope*. From what you have studied about her this week:

✣ What was her *need*?

✣ What was her *hope*?

✣ What was God's *promise*?

After sinning against Moses, Miriam's immediate need may have been the healing of her leprosy, but her greater need was the healing of her heart. Removing Miriam from the camp for 7 days gave an opportunity for that to take place. How many times had Miriam sinned in a similar way? How many times had God warned her of the consequences of this sin in smaller ways that she had not heeded?

1. 1 Corinthians 11:31 says, *"For if we would judge ourselves, we would not be judged."* What does it mean to judge ourselves?

2. Consider the difference it would have made if Miriam had judged her own sin.

3. What difference might it make in your life if you judged your own sin?

Look up the following verses and share what they teach us:

✤ Romans 2:4b

✤ Hebrews 12:6

✤ 2 Corinthians 7:10a

4. Do you think Miriam liked having a critical spirit? Do you? Share the struggles Miriam may have had with this fault in her life.

5. How did God's reaction to this sin of Miriam show how He felt about her?

6. Have you ever experienced the chastisement of God for your
    sin? What does this teach you about His feeling toward you?
    (See also Hebrews 12:8.)

We know that God was angry at the sin of Miriam and Aaron; His
Word says so. But we also know that He loved Miriam. He knew
her great need and in His chastisement of her sin, He was doing a
work in her heart. It seems probable that Miriam never sinned in
this way again and that there was a new freedom in her life after
this experience. We might say this was a case in which God took
what Satan meant for evil and used it for good!

David's testimony is this: *"In the day when I called, You answered
me; and You strengthened me with strength (might and
inflexibility to temptation) in my inner self."* Psalm 138:3
AMPLIFIED

Your Discovery

*"Call to Me, and I will answer you, and I will tell you great and mighty things, which you
do not know."* Jeremiah 33:3

Sometimes when we do a study considering a character of the
Bible, we start with a pre-conceived notion of who we think that
person is. We have heard messages or read books about them.
We already think we know them! We may have pre-set ideas
based on the way they have been portrayed to us through the
eyes of others. Hopefully this week some of your pre-conceived
notions have been changed, as you have looked at our subject
with fresh eyes, seeking the Lord for a fresh glimpse of truth.
Today we will look at what *you* have discovered or rediscovered
about our woman of the week.

1. Did you have any pre-conceived notions about Miriam? What were they?

2. Share at least one discovery or rediscovery you made about Miriam in your study this week.

3. How did this change your thoughts about her or her circumstances?

4. Is there anything that you will think or do differently as a result of what you have learned from Miriam?

5. Did you discover anything new about *yourself* this week? If so, what was it?

Your Prayer

"Search me, O God, and know my heart ..." Psalm 139:23

Compose a prayer to the Lord based on what you have gleaned from your study this week. Consider this: Is there anything you want to change in your life? Is there an attitude you realize needs adjusting? Is there a perspective that needs to be changed? Do you need to die to yourself? Do you need God's love poured into your heart for someone? Share whatever your heart is sensing with your Father in heaven who loves you and desires nothing more than to help you in your endeavor to be a godly woman.

_____
_____
_____
_____
_____
_____
_____
_____
_____
_____
_____
_____
_____
_____
_____
_____
_____
_____
_____
_____

NOTES

ABOUT THE AUTHOR

Linda has dedicated her life to serving the Lord as a teacher, writer, and speaker. While teaching the Word of God, training leaders, and speaking at retreats and other women's ministry functions, she has also written curriculum for over 20 books of the Bible.

If you would be interested in having more information about her ministry or purchase her books/Bible Studies, please visit her blog at www.lindaosborne.net, or email her at myutmost1@aol.com.

www.ingramcontent.com/pod-product-compliance
Lightning Source LLC
Chambersburg PA
CBHW060623030426
42337CB00018B/3173